The Science of Gems

Serena Hain

✳ Smithsonian

Contributing Author

Jennifer Lawson

Consultants

Jeffrey E. Post, Ph.D.
Chairman, Department of Mineral Sciences
Curator, National Gem and Mineral Collection
Smithsonian Institution

Sharon Banks
3rd Grade Teacher
Duncan Public Schools

Publishing Credits

Rachelle Cracchiolo, M.S.Ed., *Publisher*
Conni Medina, M.A.Ed., *Managing Editor*
Diana Kenney, M.A.Ed., NBCT, *Content Director*
Véronique Bos, *Creative Director*
Robin Erickson, *Art Director*
Michelle Jovin, M.A., *Associate Editor*
Mindy Duits, *Senior Graphic Designer*
Smithsonian Science Education Center

Image Credits: front cover, p.1, p.5 (top), p.22 (bottom), p.24 (right), p.25
© Smithsonian; pp.6–7 Dorling Kindersley/Science Source; p.7 (bottom) Carrie
Wallestad; p.8 (bottom) Phil Hill/Science Source; pp.8–9 Javier Trueba/MSF/Science
Source; p.10 Bloomberg/Getty Images; p.11 Olivier Polet/Corbis /GettyImages;
p.13 (top) Malcolm Fielding, The BOC Group plc/Science Source; p.15 (top) Serato/
Shutterstock; p.16 (bottom) De Agostini Editorial/Getty Images; pp.16–17 Bill
Bachmann/Science Source; p.20 Carroll Photo/Shutterstock; p.24 (left) Museo
Nacional de Historia, Chapultepec Castle, Mexico; all other images from iStock and/
or Shutterstock.

Library of Congress Cataloging-in-Publication Data

Names: Haines, Serena, author.
Title: The science of gems / Serena Haines.
Description: Huntington Beach, CA : Teacher Created Materials, 2019. |
  Audience: K to Grade 3. | Includes index. |
Identifiers: LCCN 2018030481 (print) | LCCN 2018036678 (ebook) | ISBN
  9781493869077 | ISBN 9781493866670
Subjects: LCSH: Gems--Juvenile literature. | Crystals--Juvenile literature.
Classification: LCC QE392.2 (ebook) | LCC QE392.2 .H35 2019 (print) | DDC
  553.8--dc23
LC record available at https://lccn.loc.gov/2018030481

Teacher Created Materials

5301 Oceanus Drive
Huntington Beach, CA 92649-1030
www.tcmpub.com
ISBN 978-1-4938-6667-0

Table of Contents

Minerals to Gems

Have you ever looked at a rock up close? You might see tiny flecks of color. Those are some of the **minerals** that make the rock. Some minerals can be cut and polished to make gems.

It takes a lot of work to make gems. Some people have to find minerals. Other people have to cut and polish minerals to make gems. But how do these people do their jobs? It all begins with finding minerals.

Some of these emerald minerals have been cut and polished to make gems.

The opal minerals that are part of this rock are easy to see.

How Minerals Form

Minerals are formed in rocks in three ways. The first way involves **magma**. Magma is found underground. It is made up of rocks that are so hot they have turned to liquid. Those rocks are made of minerals.

Over time, magma comes to Earth's surface. It cools as it rises. Once it cools enough, it turns solid. This forms **igneous** (IHG-nee-uhs) rocks. These rocks are made of the same minerals that the magma was.

Minerals and Crystals

Most minerals found in nature are **crystals**. Each crystal is made up of special shapes. Not all crystals are turned into gems. Salt is a mineral that is a crystal. But people do not make salt gems!

volcano

magma rising to Earth's surface

igneous rocks

buildup of hot magma

This rock is obsidian, which is an igneous rock.

The second way minerals form involves underground water. Deep within the earth, heat and pressure cause minerals to **dissolve** in water. The hot water fills cracks in rocks. Over time, the water cools. The pressure drops. Then, the minerals form into crystals in the water. The new crystals fill the cracks in the earth. Those cracks are called veins.

The third way minerals form also involves water. Some water has dissolved minerals in it. When this mineral water gets hot, it **evaporates**. That leaves just minerals behind.

A scientist in Kenya studies a vein of minerals in the earth.

A scientist studies huge crystals in Pulpí, Spain.

Working Together

Minerals can be used for many things. Scientists, builders, doctors, and other workers need minerals for their jobs. They turn to **geologists** for help finding **rare** rocks and minerals.

Gem hunters also look for minerals all over the world. These people want to find minerals that they can have polished into gems.

A gem hunter in Colombia looks for emeralds.

A gem hunter in Angola shows the diamond he has found.

How do gem hunters know whether they have found a mineral they can turn into a gem? They start by taking their rocks to people who study them. These rock scientists are called geologists. They use special tools to find out what rocks are made of. They can tell gem hunters what minerals are in each rock. That helps gem hunters know how they can use the minerals.

A geologist cracks open a rock to see its minerals.

A geologist uses a machine to study and test minerals.

Next, gem hunters go to **gemologists**. These scientists do many different jobs. Some gemologists might tell gem hunters how much money minerals are worth. Others might study and test gems. Or, they might use gems in tools. Gems are used in drills, machines, computers, and more!

A gemologist inspects a gem that has been polished and shaped.

This builder uses a tool with a diamond part to cut through a concrete wall.

Technology & Engineering

Gem Uses

Many people use gems every day. Scientists use gems in lasers. Builders use harder gems, such as diamonds, to drill and cut things. Even watches and cell phones contain gems!

Making Gems

To make gems, workers cut and polish minerals. Before they are cut and polished, minerals are called "gem roughs."

The first step is to break the rough into smaller parts. This makes them easier to handle. People use saws and rock hammers to split and break the roughs. How the final gems will be used decides how big the rough should be.

A gemologist uses a rock hammer and knife to break a rock.

This rough will be cut and polished to make a diamond gem.

A gemologist looks through an eyepiece as a saw cuts a diamond.

Scientists have identified more than 5,000 minerals. However, only about 15 of those are used to make gems for jewelry.

Next, roughs are ground into the right shapes. It is important to know what purpose a finished gem will serve. That helps people decide which shape to make it.

The next step is to **sand** the rough. This helps smooth out hard edges and scratches. It also helps to shape the rough even more.

A gem cutter grinds a diamond rough.

A boy in Ukraine learns how to sand a rough.

Cutting Gems

Many gems have tiny, flat sides. These flat sides are called facets (FA-sits). Gem cutters can make certain facets to help the gems shine. They can also use facets to make patterns on the surface of the gem.

Once a rough is the right size, it is either polished or tumbled. Polishing is used on faceted roughs. It is what makes a rough into a gem. It also makes the gem shine.

Some roughs do not have facets. For those, the final step is tumbling. Tumbling makes round, smooth gems.

A gem cutter polishes a rough.

Roughs are tumbled to make them smooth.

Counting Carats

A gem's worth depends on a few things. One of those things is its weight. A carat is the unit used to measure the weight of gems. One carat equals 200 milligrams. That is about the same weight as a raindrop!

Famous Gems

Once gems have been polished, they sparkle and shine. Some are such works of art that they become famous. Here are some of the most famous gems in the world.

Dark Jubilee Opal

The Dark Jubilee (joo-buh-LEE) Opal is a famous black opal. It is huge! It weighs more than 300 carats. It was found in Australia. That is where most opals come from.

the Dark Jubilee Opal

This boulder in Australia is made of opal minerals.

This ring has a white opal center.

Maximillian Emerald

The Maximillian Emerald is famous too. The leader of Mexico used to wear it. It is not as big as the opal. But it is famous for its deep green color.

This 1864 painting shows Emperor Maximillian I of Mexico.

the Maximillian Emerald

The Hope Diamond

Most diamonds look colorless. But the Hope Diamond is blue. That makes it rare. The Hope family used to own it. That is where it got its name. People call it the most famous diamond in the world.

the Hope Diamond

Getting Started

There are many uses for gems and minerals. People use them in labs. Some people use gems for drilling into the earth. Other people just want to have pretty jewelry!

If you want to learn about gems, start collecting rocks. Try to see what minerals they are made of. Maybe you will find the next famous gem. You just need a bit of good luck!

Some rocks are called geodes. They are hollow and lined with crystals inside.

STEAM CHALLENGE

Define the Problem

Pretend you and a friend are going gem hunting. Build a tool that will help you get rocks out of the ground to inspect their minerals.

Constraints: You may use craft sticks, tin foil, cardboard, rubber bands, plastic utensils, paper clips, and plastic cups.

Criteria: Your tool must help a gem hunter dig a rock out of a ball of mud. It must also help a gem hunter pick up the rock. Your tool must work without the user touching the mud.

Research and Brainstorm

How do scientists know where to find gems? How are gems made? What tools do geologists use to open rocks?

Design and Build

Sketch a plan for your tool. What purpose will each part serve? What materials will work best? Build the model.

Test and Improve

Use your tool to dig a rock out of a ball of mud. Then, use your tool to pick up the rock. Did it work? How can you improve it? Improve your design and try again.

Reflect and Share

What was the hardest part about building your tool? Is there another way you can test your design? How would your design change if you had to break open the rock?

Glossary

crystals—minerals that occur as shapes with flat, smooth sides

dissolve—to mix with a liquid until the solid becomes part of the liquid

evaporates—changes from a liquid into a gas

gemologists—people who inspect crystals and gems

geologists—scientists who study rocks, land, and soil to learn about the history of Earth

igneous—a type of rock formed when hot liquid rock cools and hardens

magma—hot liquid rock that is below earth's surface

minerals—substances that naturally form in the earth

rare—not common

sand—to make the surface of something smooth by rubbing it with a rough object

Index

Career Advice
from Smithsonian

Do you want to study gems?
Here are some tips to get you started.

"When I was a kid, I picked up rocks wherever I went. If you want to learn about rocks, minerals, and gems, become a geologist!"
—*Jeffrey E. Post, Chairman and Curator*

"If you love gems like I do, become a gemologist. Go to museums and learn about the gems they have on display. One day, you can teach people all about them!"
—*Christine Webb, Gemologist*